Simon COATES.

£4.60

A David Bennett Book

*This book is dedicated to my daughter Chloe,*
*and to my ginger tom-cat Alfie,*
*a never-ending source of annoyance*
*and inspiration.*

G. T.

First published in 1992 by
Kingfisher Books,
Grisewood & Dempsey Ltd,
Elsley House, 24-30 Great Titchfield Street,
London W1P 7AD

Editor: Karen Filsell
Designer: Andrew Crowson

BRITISH LIBRARY CATALOGUING IN PUBLICATION DATA
Tomblin, Gill
What do small furry animals do all day?
I. Title
599
ISBN 0 86272 679 4

Consultants: Claire Robinson,
Education Officer, London Zoo
Michael Chinery

Produced and directed by
David Bennett Books Ltd,
94 Victoria Street, St Albans,
Herts, AL1 3TG

Typesetting by Type City
Production by Imago
Printed in Singapore

# What do small, furry Animals do all day?

## GILL TOMBLIN

Kingfisher Books

Ever since I was a child, I've been curious about the everyday behaviour of animals. Why, for instance, did my pleasure-loving cat, lazing in front of the fire, suddenly go out into the cold night to yowl and hiss at another cat on the garden wall? It was only much later, of course, I learned that cats mark their territory and this is the way they defend it against intruders.

As I grew up, country walks became adventures. I loved to see if I could tell which animals had been around - footprints in mud by a river might be those of a water vole, hair caught in barbed wire might be that of a fox or badger and teeth marks in a mushroom, the sign of a wood mouse's meal.

Watching animals in the wild usually means waiting very patiently and quietly. I've sat and watched rabbits, quite unaware of my presence, nibbling the grass while one or two kept watch on their hind legs, sniffing the air. I've seen a badger at the same time every night, along one of his well-trodden routes, and I've caught fleeting glimpses of a fox returning to its den after its nightly hunt.

In Australia, where I lived for three years, I discovered possums would take nuts from my hand. They were almost as tame as grey squirrels in England which can be seen in every park, hurtling from tree to tree.

When I want to study more unusual or threatened animals, I go to wildlife sanctuaries or zoos. Here I can watch elegant lemurs being fed or see bushbabies bounding about as if they had springs on their feet. One of my favourite places is the night house, where nocturnal animals are kept in the quiet gloom. I can just see well enough to sketch how animals feed, move and relate to one another.

I never get tired of watching and sketching animals. They are endlessly fascinating and I'm always discovering something new.

Gill Tomblin

# CONTENTS

# Introduction

The small, furry animals I have chosen for this book are all mammals, a group of animals which have certain features in common. Mammals have hair and teeth, and a backbone and skeleton inside their bodies. With the exception of the platypus and the spiny anteater, which both lay eggs, all mammals give birth to live young. The mothers feed their young with their own milk, which is all the food the young need until they are ready to feed themselves. In fact, the word mammal comes from a Latin word, *mamma*, which means breast.

*raccoon*

Mammals are warm blooded animals. This means they can keep their body temperature more or less the same whatever the weather. If they get too hot, they sweat or pant to cool down. In cool weather, their hair keeps them warm. Many mammals, particularly aquatic ones, have two sorts of hair. Close to their skin, they have soft short underhair. Longer, coarser guard hairs on top trap a layer of air and stop their body heat from escaping.

*sugar glider*

*snowshoe hare*

Being warm-blooded enables mammals to live in almost every habitat on Earth - from the icy Arctic to hot deserts and steamy rainforests - wherever they can find a good supply of food. Mammals need to eat regularly so they have enough energy to keep themselves warm.

*flying squirrel*

Just by looking at a mammal, it is possible to tell quite a lot about where it lives and its habits. Mammals that live in trees, for example, usually have specially adapted limbs for climbing and gripping. Aquatic mammals on the other hand usually have streamlined bodies, powerful tails and webbed feet. Many nocturnal animals have big eyes or ears to help them find food in the dark. Meat-eaters have sharp teeth for biting and tearing flesh; plant-eaters have blunt teeth for grinding plants.

*grey squirrel*

*douroucouli*

There are more than four thousand different kinds of living mammals. Scientists have divided them into groups which have similar features, such as pouches, wings or grasping fingers. These groups are called orders and the different kinds of animals in each order are called species. For this book, I have chosen a few of my favourite species from the following orders:

**Monotremes** are mammals which lay soft-shelled eggs and have no teeth. There are only three living species of monotremes: the platypus, the long-beaked spiny anteater and the short-beaked spiny anteater.

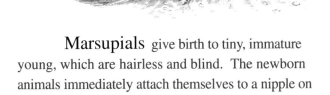

*platypus*

**Marsupials** give birth to tiny, immature young, which are hairless and blind. The newborn animals immediately attach themselves to a nipple on the mother's belly and stay there until they are fully formed. Most marsupials have a pouch for their young.

*Virginia opossum*

**Insectivores** are small, active, mainly nocturnal animals. They have small eyes and poor sight, but long, narrow sensitive snouts and a good sense of smell. They have many sharp, pointed teeth and feed mainly on insects and other invertebrates.

*common shrew*

**Bats** are the only mammals capable of true flight. The wings of bats are modified hands - the arm and finger bones are very elongated to support the wing membranes. There are almost a thousand species of bats - nearly one quarter of all mammal species.

*pipistrelle*

**Primates** are mostly tree-dwelling, sharp-sighted, intelligent mammals found mainly in tropical rainforests. They nearly all have flexible, grasping hands and feet. They also have bigger brains and live longer than most other mammals. Their young grow slowly and are dependent upon their parents for a relatively long time. Human beings are included in this order.

*slow loris*

**Lagomorphs** are ground-living animals with large ears and wide set eyes. They are all herbivores and have two pairs of upper incisor teeth.

*European brown hare*

**Rodents** make up nearly 40% of all mammal species and are found worldwide. They are mostly small and have frequent, large litters. Rodents have large, chisel-edged incisors, which grow continuously.

*house mouse*

**Carnivores** are mainly predatory meat-eating mammals. They have keen eyesight, hearing or sense of smell to help them find prey, and they can move quickly to catch it. Carnivores generally have large, pointed canine teeth and sharp molars for holding and slicing meat.

*European wild cat*

9

Monotremes

# PLATYPUS

*broad, furry tail
stores fat*

*burrow entrance*

*water-repellent fur*

50cm (20in)
head to tail

*sensitive, rubbery bill
for finding prey*

The platypus is an unusual mammal.
It lays eggs like reptiles and birds
instead of giving birth to live young,
but it is warm-blooded and hairy,
and the mother suckles her babies
on milk like other mammals.
The platypus lives in the rivers of
eastern Australia and Tasmania.
Its streamlined body is well adapted
for swimming, since it finds its food
underwater.  It builds a burrow in
a riverbank where it lives alone.

When courting, platypuses swim
around in circles.  The male tries
to catch the female's tail in his bill.

The female builds a nest where
she lays two soft-shelled eggs.
She wraps her body around
them to keep them warm.

After ten days, the eggs hatch.  Baby
platypuses suck the milk that oozes through
pores in their mother's belly.  They learn to
swim when they are four months old.

7.5m (25ft)

*breeding burrow plugged with earth for safety*

10

At dawn and dusk, the platypus comes out of its burrow to feed on crayfish and insect larvae. It can stay underwater without breathing for up to ten minutes.

*tail used as rudder*

*hind feet used for steering*

*front feet used as paddles*

Because its eyes and ears are shut underwater, the platypus finds food by feeling in the mud with its bill. It brings its food up to the surface to eat.

The platypus grooms itself standing up. Its tail helps it to balance.

On land, the platypus walks on its knuckles.

*webbed front paw used for swimming*

*claws of front paw come out for digging on land*

*hind foot of male with poisoned spur for self-defence*

The adult has no teeth. Inside its mouth, it has cheek pouches and ridged pads for chewing food.

11

# KOALA

Koalas are found in Australia, where they live in the branches of eucalyptus trees. They sleep eighteen hours a day and feed mainly at night. They are very picky eaters, and choose only particular kinds of eucalyptus leaves. The female koala gives birth to one baby each year. A newborn koala is the size of a fingernail. It crawls into a pouch on its mother's belly and stays there for six months, feeding and growing. It lives with its mother until it is one year old.

*thick fur on back for extra warmth in windy treetops*

*tufted ears*

*big sensitive nose for sniffing leaves*

**NEW SOUTH WALES KOALA**

Koalas eat about 1kg (2lb) of eucalyptus leaves each day. They rarely drink, because they get enough water from the leaves.

Sometimes, a baby koala will cling tightly to its mother if she leaps from tree to tree.

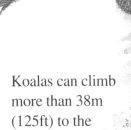

*hand*

*claws used as comb for grooming*

*foot with opposable big toe*

*two opposable thumbs, and claws for firm grip*

Koalas can climb more than 38m (125ft) to the top of a tree.

12

Marsupials

# POSSUM and GLIDER

*large ears and eyes*

*long, sharp claws for gripping branches*

*body length 60cm (24in)*

Possums and gliders are Australian nocturnal tree dwellers, which have strong hands and feet. Possums also have prehensile tails which help them move easily through the trees.

### BRUSH-TAILED POSSUM

The brush-tailed possum lives in woodlands, where it sleeps during the day in tree hollows. At night, it feeds on leaves, buds, insects and small animals.

The baby brush-tailed possum clings to the nipple in its mother's pouch until it is five months old.

### SUGAR GLIDER

A sugar glider gets its name because it feeds on the sweet blossoms of eucalyptus trees. When it leaps into the air, the skin between its front and hind legs stretches out like a parachute. Its tail is used for balance and steering.

### HONEY POSSUM

The tiny honey possum reaches inside flowers with its long, bristly tongue and licks up nectar and pollen.

*body length 8cm (3in)*

Marsupials

# WOMBAT

The wombat spends the day asleep in a burrow near the edge of a forest. At night it grazes, or digs for roots. It is well-adapted for surviving on a poor diet in times of drought.

**HAIRY NOSED WOMBAT**

*long, silky fur*

*good hearing*

*teeth grow all the time, but are constantly worn down by gnawing*

*pouch opens backwards to prevent baby from being hit by flying earth*

*body length up to 1.2m (47in)*

*strong paws for digging*

# NUMBAT

The numbat hunts for termites, catching thousands of them each day. It lives and hunts alone.

The numbat does not have a pouch for its babies. Instead, they hang on teats on their mother's stomach.

*striped and spotted coat providing camouflage in the woods*

*body length up to 27cm (11in)*

*sharp claws for ripping logs open*

At the sound of danger, the numbat stands upright and gets ready to run.

*pointed snout and long, sticky tongue for reaching termites*

14

Marsupials

# OPOSSUM

**VIRGINIA OPOSSUM**

The Virginia opossum is the only marsupial in North America. It is slow-moving, like most nocturnal animals. Its toes and tail make it a good climber. The Virginia opossum nests in tree hollows, in rock crevices or under fallen logs. It eats almost anything - birds, insects, fruit, worms and even the contents of dustbins.

*nest*

*body length up to 50cm (20in)*

*hand with sharp claws for gripping bark*

*foot with opposable big toe*

*long, silky fur*

When faced with danger from a dog or a fox, the Virginia opossum 'plays dead', sometimes for hours. Its predator usually loses interest.

Baby opossums cling to their mother's back for a month after leaving her pouch.

Up to twenty young are born at one time, but half of them die on the way to their mother's pouch. If the pouch is too crowded, a teat may be pulled outside, like this.

Opossums have prehensile tails.

15

# SHREW

*body length up to 8cm (3in)*

*long snout*

*sensitive whiskers*

Shrews are solitary animals. They search day and night for food. They use up so much energy that they must eat every two to three hours or they will die. Shrews have very poor eyesight, so they use their whiskers and good sense of smell to find food.

**EUROPEAN WATER SHREW**

*feet with stiff hairs for trapping water to make them like paddles*

*bristly tail helps shrew steer in water*

A shrew builds a burrow in a riverbank, often with an underwater entrance.

As a wet shrew runs through the narrow tunnels of its burrow, its fur is squeezed dry and groomed.

Freshwater snail shells and caddis fly cases are signs that a water shrew has been feeding.

A shrew has sharp teeth and poisonous saliva. Its bite paralyses prey.

Underwater, the shrew is very buoyant because air is trapped under its fur. It paddles hard to catch its prey.

The common shrew finds food among leaves and in tunnels that it digs underground. It eats worms, caterpillars, spiders, beetles and woodlice.

*body length*
*6cm (2.5in)*

**COMMON SHREW**

The shrew uses its claws and teeth for grooming. In spring, it sheds its dark winter fur and grows a shorter, light-coloured summer coat.

The female builds a nest inside a burrow. Each year she has one or more litters of four to seven young.

Before they become independent, young shrews follow their mother by forming a chain.

Each common shrew has its own feeding territory which it defends fiercely from other hungry shrews. A shrew advances on any intruder until their whiskers touch. If the intruder does not retreat, both shrews stand up and squeak.

After that, they roll on to their backs, wriggling, squeaking, and grabbing for each other's tail. They do not really hurt each other.

Finally, one shrew gives up and runs away.

17

Insectivores
# MOLE

*sensitive tail*

Moles are found in Europe, Asia and North America. They live almost entirely underground, and are especially well-suited for burrowing. Their shoulders and forefeet are very powerful, with strong, pointed claws. Their fur is so short that it can lie in any direction. This means a mole can move equally well forwards or backwards in its tunnels, and can even roll over to change direction.

*very poor eyesight*

*body length 13cm (5in)*

*velvety fur*

*long snout and whiskers help find earthworms by touch*

## EUROPEAN MOLE

The female enlarges one of her tunnels to build a breeding nest, which she lines with leaves and grass. Three or four young are born there in the spring.

*forearm has extra finger-like bone for digging*

*large fortress molehill covering breeding nest*

*molehills*

*nest has several exits*

Moles hunt and feed for four hours, rest for another four hours, and then go hunting again.

*store of live worms, heads bitten off by mole*

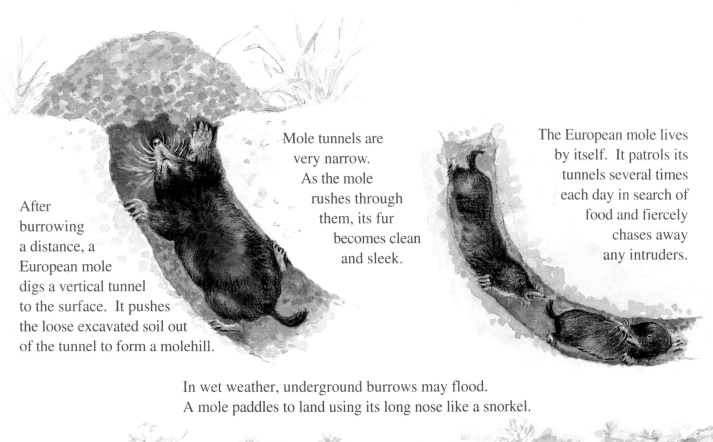

After burrowing a distance, a European mole digs a vertical tunnel to the surface. It pushes the loose excavated soil out of the tunnel to form a molehill.

Mole tunnels are very narrow. As the mole rushes through them, its fur becomes clean and sleek.

The European mole lives by itself. It patrols its tunnels several times each day in search of food and fiercely chases away any intruders.

In wet weather, underground burrows may flood.
A mole paddles to land using its long nose like a snorkel.

## NORTH AMERICAN STAR-NOSED MOLE

The American star-nosed mole swims well and catches most of its food in the water. It feeds on shrimps, small fish, insect larvae, and earthworms.

*long tail*

*body length up to 20cm (8in)*

The mole has a ring of twenty-two tentacles around its snout, which it waves around in search of food.

*underwater entrance to burrow*

# BAT

*free thumb
with claw*

Bats are found in all parts of the world except cold polar regions, and there are over 950 species of them. They are all nocturnal and are the only mammals that can fly. Fruit bats live in tropical countries and use their large eyes to find their way about. Insect-eating bats live in temperate and tropical countries. They have large ears and catch insects using echolocation. There are also bats which catch fish, hunt rodents or drink the blood of large mammals.

## GREY-HEADED FRUIT BAT

The fruit bat pierces the skin of ripe bananas, dates, guavas and figs with its sharp teeth. Then it sucks out the flesh.

## PIPISTRELLE

Pipistrelle bats usually have one young at a time. The young bat clings to its mother as she flies, until it becomes too heavy for her.

Many mothers and babies hang together in nursery roosts inside buildings or caves, or on trees.

*body length 5cm (2in)*

*wingspan
23cm (9in)*

By hooking its thumbs into tree bark and pushing with its feet, the bat can crawl along a branch or even up a vertical tree trunk.

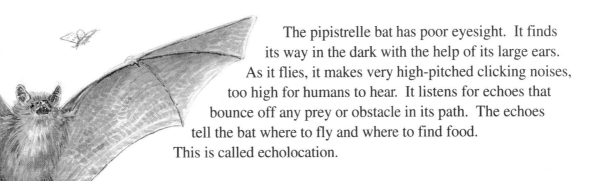

The pipistrelle bat has poor eyesight. It finds its way in the dark with the help of its large ears. As it flies, it makes very high-pitched clicking noises, too high for humans to hear. It listens for echoes that bounce off any prey or obstacle in its path. The echoes tell the bat where to fly and where to find food. This is called echolocation.

The pipistrelle flies with fast, fluttery movements in search of flying insects, usually gnats or moths.

The pipistrelle catches only one insect at a time, either in its mouth, or by scooping it up with its tail and bending over to eat it.

In winter, when insects are scarce, pipistrelle bats hibernate in cool places. Their body temperature drops until beads of condensation form on their fur.

## GREATER HORSESHOE BAT

This bat squeaks through its nostrils, which act like a megaphone.

## LONG-EARED BAT

*tragus - a fleshy spine in each ear - helps hearing*

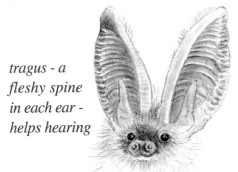

The long ears of this bat help it echolocate especially well.

## SANBORN'S LONG-NOSED BAT

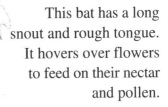

This bat has a long snout and rough tongue. It hovers over flowers to feed on their nectar and pollen.

Primates
# LEMUR

Lemurs live only in the forests of Madagascar, an island near East Africa. There are over twenty kinds. The ring-tailed lemur is one of the most common. It is about the size of a domestic cat. Ring-tails live in family groups headed by females. The females may stay together for many years. Ring-tails forage for fruit and leaves to eat. They sleep in the trees at night.

### RING-TAILED LEMUR

On the ground, a ring-tail keeps its tail in the air like a flag. This lets the rest of the group know where it is.

*tamarind fruit -
a favourite food
of all lemurs*

A young ring-tail uses its tail to hold tight to its mother, while she uses hers as a blanket.

A ring-tail's arms and legs are nearly the same length, so that it can run along the ground on all fours.

The mother carries her baby on her back wherever she goes for about six months.

During the mating season, two ring-tails may have a stink fight for a female. Each male rubs his wrists against smelly glands in his armpits and then along his tail. The two rivals then fan each other with their smelly tails.

One male may give in, or a fierce fight may follow to see who will win the female.

*sharp claw used as earpick*

*foot*

*short nails for picking fruit*

*hand*

Ring-tails have strong, nimble hands and feet, both with opposable thumbs.

Ring-tails often sit upright on the ground to sunbathe. They usually sit in groups.

# NEW WORLD MONKEYS

New World monkeys live high in the trees of South American rainforests. Because they are small, light and very agile, they are ideally suited for climbing and leaping. They have good eyesight and can spot the flowers, fruit and nuts they eat from far away. They are mainly active in the day, when they can see where they are going.

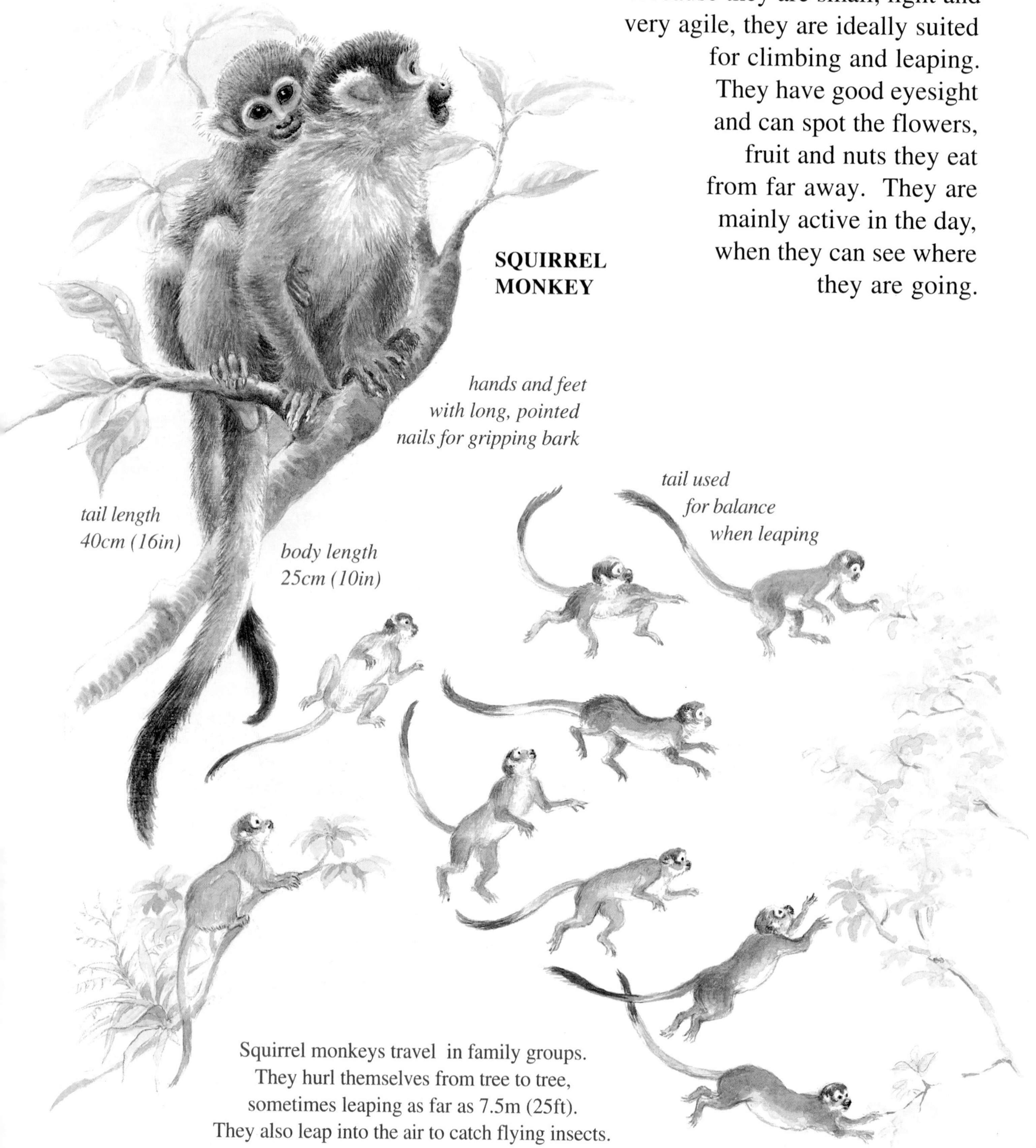

**SQUIRREL MONKEY**

*hands and feet with long, pointed nails for gripping bark*

*tail used for balance when leaping*

*tail length 40cm (16in)*

*body length 25cm (10in)*

Squirrel monkeys travel in family groups. They hurl themselves from tree to tree, sometimes leaping as far as 7.5m (25ft). They also leap into the air to catch flying insects.

24

**SPIDER MONKEY**

The underside of a prehensile tail has no hair. It has a ridged surface that can grip branches just like a hand.

Like most New World monkeys, the spider monkey can hang by its prehensile tail.

The female has one baby at a time, which rides on her back until it is independent.

*curved hands and long thin toes for grasping branches*

*body length up to 65cm (26in)*

The hand of a spider monkey is unusual because it has no thumb.

*foot*

*hand*

**CAPUCHIN MONKEY**

Like all monkeys, capuchin monkeys spend a lot of time carefully grooming their young to keep them clean.

**DOUROUCOULI**

The douroucouli is the only nocturnal monkey. It can see three times as well as humans in the dark.

25

# TAMARIN and MARMOSET

Tamarins and marmosets are very small, rare monkeys which live in the rainforests of South America. They are slim, agile climbers with sharp claws on their hands and feet. During the day they can be very vocal, producing high-pitched calls. They eat insects, fruit and flowers.

**GOLDEN LION TAMARIN**

*thick golden fur - one of the most brightly coloured mammals*

*slender fingers with sharp claws used for gripping bark*

Newborn tamarins cling to their father's fur.

*long tail for balance*

Tamarins live in family groups with a mother, father and their offspring. The father takes care of the young most of the time. He hands them over to the mother when it is time for feeding.

*body length 20cm (8in)*

26

# COMMON MARMOSET

Marmosets are great leapers.

*body length 20 cm (8in)*

A young marmoset rides on its father's back.
At two months, it can travel on its own.

During the day,
marmosets rest along branches.
At night, they sleep in holes in tree trunks.

Marmosets and tamarins hang upside down by digging their claws into branches.

Males are aggressive when defending their territory.
They arch their backs and bare their teeth to keep other males away.

The hand has long fingers and sharp claws.

Marmosets use their claws and teeth to groom each other.

*hand*

*foot*

The foot has a short big toe with a flattish nail. The rest of the toes have claws.

27

# BUSHBABY

Bushbabies live in Africa. They are so named because they have a cry like a human baby. They rest all day in groups, curled up on a branch or in a nest of leaves. At night, they split up and hunt alone for insects, lizards and birds' eggs. They also eat fruit and sip tree sap.

*large folding ears*

*large eyes*

*hand*

*flattened fingers for climbing and grasping*

**SENEGAL BUSHBABY**

*body length 40cm (16in) including tail*

A bushbaby is a fast and agile leaper. It has strong hind legs and can leap up to 6m (18ft) between trees. Its long tail helps it to balance and brake. It lands upright, gripping the tree trunk.

*strong furred tail used as a rudder for steering*

Bushbabies use their incredibly sharp hearing to find insects in the dark.

The mother carries her baby around on her back. Occasionally, she carries it in her mouth. After a few weeks, she leaves it in the nest while she hunts.

# LORIS

*thick, woolly fur*    *large eyes*

Lorises are nocturnal animals that live in the tropical forests of Asia. They stay high up in the trees, rarely coming down to the ground. They creep slowly along branches in search of insects, trying not to shake twigs or leaves which might give them away. Lorises have very short tails that are hidden under their thick fur. Since they move so slowly, they do not need a long tail for balance.

**SLOW LORIS**

*strong, muscular legs and feet*

*body length 38cm (15in)*

The mother parks her baby on a branch while she hunts.

Lorises eat many bad-tasting caterpillars and other insects that most animals won't touch. They creep towards their prey until it is within reach and then suddenly lunge forward to grasp it.

*hand with opposable thumb*

Lorises drink dew by wiping their fingers along wet leaves and then licking them.

Lorises have a network of blood vessels in their limbs which slow down the blood flow. This means they can remain still for hours at a time.

# RABBIT

Rabbits are found in many parts of the world. They usually eat grasses, but will also eat other plant matter, such as twigs and bark. Some rabbits live alone or in small groups, making their homes in forms on the ground. Others live in large groups in underground warrens.

**EUROPEAN RABBIT**

*soft, dense fur*

*long, mobile ears for sharp hearing*

European rabbits come out to feed at dawn and dusk, rarely moving far from the warren.

*large, widely-spaced eyes for all-round vision*

*body length 40cm (16in)*

*short tail*

Young rabbits, called kittens, are born naked and blind. They emerge from their nest at three weeks, fully furred.

*breeding nest lined with fur from doe*

*sleeping burrow*

*rabbit warren*

A rabbit stands on its hind legs to get a better view. It turns its head from side to side to catch the scent, sight or sound of any predators.

At the first sign of a predator, such as a stoat or fox, rabbits dash for their burrows. They flash the white underside of their tails to warn other rabbits of the danger.

A rabbit moves in a series of short leaps with one forefoot slightly in front of the other. Its powerful hind legs are much longer than the forelegs.

*tracks of forefeet*　　*tracks of hind feet*

Rabbits digest their food twice to get all the nutrients from it. A rabbit swallows the first set of soft droppings it passes, and then leaves a second set of hard, dark droppings outside the burrow entrance.

European rabbits often damage trees by eating the bark. Often they eat the bark all the way around young trees, causing them to die.

A male rabbit, called a buck, marks his territory by rubbing the ground with the scent gland on his chin.

**MARSH COTTONTAIL**

**EASTERN COTTONTAIL**

The Eastern cottontail is found in much of Central and North America. It rests in a form in the grass. When in danger, the cottontail sometimes finds safety in the disused burrow of another animal.

The marsh cottontail rabbit makes a nest in marshy areas. It can swim well and if threatened, lies motionless on its back in the water. Only its eyes, nose and mouth remain above the surface.

*walking tracks of a marsh cottontail*

Lagomorphs
# HARE

*long ears*

*form*

*powerful hind legs*

Brown hares are solitary, cautious animals. They live unsheltered in open pastures. Their only protection is their form, which they make in long grass. Brown hares have thick fur which keeps them warm. Sharp hearing and eyesight keep them alert to danger, and they can run very fast to escape.

**EUROPEAN BROWN HARE**

*body length 60cm (24in)*

A brown hare lies motionless, hiding from danger.

Males, called jacks, compete for females in spring. They turn in circles and box each other with their paws until one of them gives up.

Brown hares usually have two young in a litter, but may have three litters in a year. The young, called leverets, are born fully furred and with their eyes open.

If a brown hare sights a hawk, it runs away as fast as it can. It can run as fast as 56km/h (35mph).

When the hawk swoops down, the hare suddenly jumps out of the way and the bird crash-lands. Hares can jump as high as 2m (6ft).

*skull of a European hare*

Brown hares feed mainly at dusk and dawn on grass and vegetables. They eat their first set of soft droppings to give them extra nutrients.

*large incisors with a space behind for carrying food and bedding*

**SNOWSHOE HARE**

In spring, the snowshoe hare loses its white coat and grows a reddish-brown coat for the summer.

The snowshoe hare lives in Canada and the northern United States. In winter, it feeds on twigs and bark, and roots that it finds beneath the snow.

The soles of the hind feet are covered with thick hair to help grip snow. These 'snowshoes' also keep the hare's feet warm.

# BEAVER

*sharp teeth for gnawing wood*

*body length up to 1.2m (46in)*

*flat, scaly tail for steering*

Beavers live by riverbanks in the forests of North America and parts of Europe. They are aquatic rodents that are well-known for their building skills. With their sharp teeth they gnaw down trees and cut up logs to build dams and homes called lodges. Beavers live in family groups made up of parents and offspring. The young, known as kits, leave to make their own homes after about two years.

## NORTH AMERICAN BEAVER

Beavers build their lodges near alder, poplar, willow and aspen trees, which grow by riverbanks. They use bigger, older branches for building, and eat the shoots and bark of young branches.

*lodge*

*winter stockpile of twigs pushed firmly into mud*

*underwater entrance to living chamber*

*dam made of logs, twigs and mud creating a pond for the lodge*

Beavers dig canals from their lodges so they can fetch wood from further afield when their local supply runs out.

The beaver slaps its tail against the water to warn other beavers when predators threaten the lodge or the kits.

*tail raised to change direction*

*webbed hind feet for speed underwater*

A beaver can stay below the surface for fifteen minutes before coming up to breathe. Its eyes are protected by a transparent skin so it can see underwater.

*forefeet tucked under chin while swimming*

A beaver gnaws all around a tree trunk and then runs out of the way when the tree falls. It may be crushed if it is not quick enough. It gnaws the branches into small lengths for building and eating.

*hind foot*

*forefoot*

*skull showing large incisors protected by extra-hard, rusty-coloured enamel*

A beaver can close its lips behind its incisors, so that it can gnaw and carry sticks underwater without choking.

A beaver stands upright to carry a tired kit.

Young kits cannot dive. Instead, they ride on their mother's back.

# TREE SQUIRREL

*drey*

Grey squirrels spend much of their time scurrying about in the treetops, feeding on nuts, shoots and fruits. At night, and in cold and rainy weather, they rest in a nest, called a drey, made of leaves, twigs and bark. Grey squirrels are native to the eastern United States. They were introduced to Britain a hundred years ago and are now a familiar sight in parks and gardens.

### GREY SQUIRREL

The female grey squirrel lines the drey with soft leaves and moss. Her young are born there naked, blind and deaf.

*body length up to 50cm (20in) including tail*

*wide-angle vision*

*powerful hind legs and long hind feet for climbing*

*keen sense of smell*

*sharp claws*

*tail used as rudder*

The grey squirrel bounds from branch to branch quickly and easily. When it leaps to the ground, it lands on its forefeet and its tail flips overhead.

*hazelnut opened roughly by young grey squirrel*

Grey squirrels strip the bark from trees and feed on the sappy wood underneath.

*hazelnut opened cleanly by adult grey squirrel*

Grey squirrels hide nuts and seeds for the winter. They may also raid bird tables in the cold weather when food is scarce.

Rodents

# FLYING SQUIRREL

Flying squirrels are the only nocturnal squirrels. There are over three dozen species of them found in the forests of North America, Europe, Japan and south-east Asia. Their front and hind legs are connected by a furry fold of skin on either side of the body. When the squirrel leaps, it stretches out its limbs and the skin acts like a parachute, enabling the squirrel to glide 30 metres (100 feet) or more through the air.

**NORTHERN FLYING SQUIRREL**

*feathery tail for balance and steering*

Flying squirrels rest in tree hollows during the day. In winter, several rest together to keep warm.

A young squirrel often falls when learning to glide. The mother rescues it, picking it up by its fold of skin.

*cocked head*

*limbs outstretched in flight*

*tail raised and body upright, ready to land*

*landing on all fours, clawed toes grasping the bark*

*body length 37cm (14in) including tail*

Before the squirrel takes off, it cocks its head from side to side to judge the distance to its landing spot. Then it pushes away from the tree with its back legs, leaps into the air, and spreads its limbs out wide.

In the autumn, flying squirrels store nuts by wedging them into tree crevices.

*darting around to far side of tree in case a predator is watching*

# PRAIRIE DOG

The prairie dog's name comes from its call, which sounds like the bark of a dog, but prairie dogs are actually ground-living squirrels. They live on the grassy plains of North America in huge 'towns', each with as many as one thousand prairie dogs. Each town is divided into family units, called coteries, made up of one male, several females, and their pups. Each coterie has its own burrows with several entrances. Coteries are passed from one generation to the next.

blunt nose

small ears
for ease in
tunnelling

body length up to
42cm (16in)

volcano-shaped
burrow entrance

shorter tail
than tree squirrel
because ground-living

**BLACK-TAILED PRAIRIE DOG**

Mounds of earth at burrow
entrances serve as lookout posts
and help to prevent flooding.

coterie members on watch
at burrow entrances

guard sounding
alarm at approach
of hawk

listening
post

chamber used
during floods

sleeping chamber

latrine

carrying
bedding

Prairie dogs maintain the mounds around their burrows. Nose prints can be seen where they have pressed down the soil.

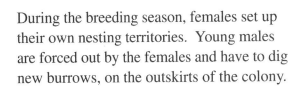

During the breeding season, females set up their own nesting territories. Young males are forced out by the females and have to dig new burrows, on the outskirts of the colony.

Sometimes a badger and a coyote work together to capture a prairie dog. One animal flushes it from the burrow. The other waits quietly nearby to catch it.

*tail flips up while calling*

A prairie dog has different calls for different predators. Once danger is past, it jumps up to give an all clear call.

Prairie dog pups learn how to kiss and nuzzle every prairie dog they meet, so that they can recognise the smell of members of their family.

# DESERT RODENTS

Rodents are the most common desert mammals. They are largely nocturnal, and rest in burrows during the day to avoid the extreme heat. They do not need to drink very much because their bodies can conserve the moisture they get from their food.

### DESERT JERBOA

*large ears and earbones amplify sound*

*sand-coloured fur providing camouflage*

*long tail for better balance on two feet*

*short forefeet with claws*

*very long hind legs for jumping*

*hair on underside of foot prevents sinking in sand*

*very large feet for bouncing*

*emergency exits*

*main entrance*

The desert jerboa lives in African and Asian deserts. Each jerboa digs its own burrow. The main entrance is blocked with sand to keep out the hot dry air and conserve moisture.

## MONGOLIAN GERBIL

This species of gerbil has become a popular pet.

Males stand on their hind legs to fight over territory.

Mongolian gerbils are sociable and share a burrow. The moisture from their breath collects in their chamber and prevents it from drying out.

## KANGAROO RAT

Kangaroo rats live in the deserts of North America, where they often fall prey to owls and snakes. Their hearing is four times sharper than human hearing. At the faintest sound, they jump for safety. They can jump as far as 4.5m (15ft) in one second.

If a kangaroo rat hears a predator, it takes off, its tail streaming downward.

It can change direction in mid-air, using its tail as a rudder.

As the rat lands, it raises its tail, which acts like a brake.

To keep its fur clean and free from parasites, the kangaroo rat takes regular sand baths.

*body length 25cm (10 in) including tail*

The kangaroo rat has fur-lined cheek pouches. On foraging trips, it picks up seeds with its front paws, and fills its pouches.

During the day, the kangaroo rat rests in a burrow mound. The entrances are plugged for safety and to keep the air inside moist and cool.

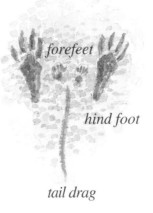

*forefeet*

*hind foot*

*tail drag*

*track of hopping kangaroo rat*

*lower bones of rat's hind feet, fused together for strength and support when jumping*

Back at its burrow, the kangaroo rat squeezes its cheeks to release the food.

Rodents
# MOUSE

*large, erect ears*

*large eyes*

*wide feet*

*long tail for balance*

*carrying a leaf to the nest for use as bedding*

*jumping tracks in the snow*

*hind feet*

*forefeet*

*tail drag*

*plum stone neatly opened by a wood mouse*

There are many species of mice, found all over the world. All of them are active and inquisitive. They generally breed frequently, and can have several litters in a year. Mice mainly eat seeds, roots, grasses and berries, though some also eat insects or worms.

## WOOD MOUSE

*body length 18cm (7in) including tail*

*a wood mouse's burrow*

*food store*

During the day, the wood mouse rests in an underground burrow.

*breeding nest*

Babies are born mainly in spring and summer, with as many as five or six in a litter.

## NORTH AMERICAN WHITE-FOOTED MOUSE

North American white-footed mice make their homes in any hidden places, such as an old bird's nest.

## HOUSE MOUSE

*nest of newspaper*

The female may have up to ten litters of three to five young each year.

*body length 10cm (4in)*

House mice are found wherever humans live, and where there is plenty of food and shelter.

If house mice are overcrowded, they become very aggressive, and males will fight for dominance.

## EUROPEAN HARVEST MOUSE

The tiny, nimble harvest mouse lives among the tall grasses of fields and meadows. In early summer, it builds a nest above the ground, safe from predators. It eats flowers, fruit, seeds and grains.

*cowslip*

*body length 13cm (5 in) including tail*

The harvest mouse grips a stalk with its hind feet and prehensile tail, to leave its forefeet free for feeding.

First the mouse shreds the ends of grass blades which are still attached to their stems.

Then it weaves the blades into a tight ball, firmly attached to the stems of grass either side

Rodents
# RAT

There are several hundred species of rats living in every part of the world except the polar regions. They breed rapidly - a single brown rat can have up to fifty young in a year, and her young can breed when they are only three months old.

## EASTERN WOODRAT

*large eyes and ears*

*furry tail*

*forefoot*

*long whiskers*

*hind foot*

*body length 46cm (18in) including tail*

The Eastern woodrat lives in North America and Mexico. It builds its nest out of all kinds of strange objects, such as bottle tops, tin cans, bones and even spoons.

## BROWN RAT

Brown rats are often found in urban areas, and are probably the most adaptable animals ever. They are excellent swimmers and many live in city sewers. In the country, they sometimes build burrows in riverbanks.

Brown rats live wherever they can find plenty of food, water and shelter. They will eat almost anything, but they test small amounts of unfamiliar food to make sure it is safe to eat.

A family of brown rats shares a scent which they transfer to one another. First one rat sniffs another, then it creeps under the other's raised leg.

Rodents
# VOLE

*small ears
hidden in fur*

Voles are small, scurrying animals that are active day and night, alternating between feeding and resting. They have many predators and rarely survive longer than a year or two.

## EUROPEAN BANK VOLE

The tiny bank vole lives in woodlands and hedgerows, where it finds shelter in the thick undergrowth.

*body length
10cm (4in)*

*short legs*

The bank vole climbs bushes and brambles to feed on fruits, seeds, leaves and flowers. It also eats insects.

*nuts hollowed out
by bank vole*

*nest*

*food
store*

The young are born blind and naked. They spend their first few weeks in an underground nest lined with grass, moss and wool.

## EUROPEAN WATER VOLE

The water vole lives on riverbanks, and feeds on grasses and other plants. It digs a burrow in the bank where it sleeps and stores food.

*footprints*

*chewed
grasses*

*body length 20cm (8in)*

Carnivores
# Fox

*pointed ears*

**RED FOX**

*eyes adapted
for night vision*

Red foxes are resourceful animals,
common in North America, Europe,
Asia and Australia. Although they are
wild animals, they sometimes live near
people. Adult red foxes live in pairs,
or in groups with one male, called a dog
fox, and several females, called vixens.

*den*

*bushy tail with
scent gland*

The vixen gives birth in
a den built underground.
The dog fox brings
food to her.

Some vixens have no young,
but help look after the cubs
of other vixens.

Older cubs follow their parents on foraging trips.
They learn how to find earthworms by sniffing
the grass, then
pulling out
the worms.

If she senses danger, the vixen
carries young cubs by the scruff
of the neck to a safe den.

46

Red foxes may come into suburban gardens and search in dustbins for scraps to eat.

Red foxes follow the same paths every night in search of food. They leave fresh droppings as scent markers.

Dog foxes sometimes fight for dominance. They stand on their hind legs and push one another, barking loudly. The fights rarely end in bloodshed.

*body length 1m (40in) including tail*

When a red fox hears the rustling of a mouse or vole, it leaps into the air and pins the prey down.

Extra food is often buried in a hole that a red fox digs with its forepaws. The fox may return to the hole when food is scarce.

# MEERKAT

good eyesight
and sense
of smell

slender body covered
with long, soft fur

striped fur on back

tapered tail

short legs

Meerkats inhabit the dry, sandy plains of southern Africa. They live in colonies and dig burrows with lots of entrances and deep passageways. Meerkats come out of their burrows at daybreak to feed, but never wander far from home. When the local food supply runs out, the whole colony moves to new feeding grounds and digs new burrows.

## SLENDER-TAILED MEERKAT

Meerkats stand on their hind legs to look over tall grasses for possible predators.

A litter of three or four young is born in a grass-lined nest in the burrow. Newborn meerkats are blind and have no fur. After a month, the babies come out of the burrow.

The whole family looks after the young meerkats. Older brothers and sisters play with them. The mother and father groom and protect the young, and take them on foraging trips to teach them which foods to eat.

Meerkats go foraging in small groups. They scrape the earth in search of centipedes, insects, spiders, lizards and roots. They make purring sounds to keep in touch with each other.

*ears that close to keep sand out*

When a meerkat spots dangerous prey, it moves forward with its back arched and its tail in the air. It can be very aggressive and can kill a small mammal or snake with its bite.

If a meerkat catches a scorpion, it bites off its stinging tail before killing and eating it.

*body length 55cm (22in) including tail*

Meerkats spend much of the day basking in the sun. When they get too hot, they lie face down in a cool burrow.

*hawk*

A few meerkats keep watch for predators, such as hawks and eagles. They stand as high up as possible so they have a good view. At the first sight of danger, the guards let out a shrill bark, and all the meerkats dash for their burrows.

# BADGER

Badgers are squat, powerful animals with strong claws for digging. Eurasian badgers live in family groups. They build deep burrow systems, called setts, in woody areas where trees and shrubs provide plenty of cover. At dusk, they come out to feed. Earthworms are their main diet, but they also eat small animals, fruit, bulbs and other plants.

**EURASIAN BADGER**

well-trodden paths to feeding grounds

sharpening claws

cubs playing by sett entrance

black and white head markings for recognition in the dark

coarse grey hair

dung-pits marking edge of territory

blunt snout, good sense of smell

old bedding

short forelegs and long, sturdy claws for digging

A litter of one to four cubs is born between January and March. The cubs stay underground for eight weeks.

stored bedding

sleeping chamber

breeding chamber

Eurasian badgers are wary of people, but they will sometimes go into gardens at night if food is provided for them. They especially like honey, peanuts and raisins.

Eurasian badgers raise their tails to spread scent on each other. The scent helps them to identify those in their group.

*body length
87cm (34in)
including tail*

Males may attack strangers venturing on to their territory. An angry badger bares its teeth and fluffs up its fur, which makes it look bigger.

## AMERICAN BADGER

An American badger defends itself by blocking the entrance to its burrow with its wide body. It uses its claws to fight off attackers.

American badgers have flatter bodies than Eurasian badgers, and their head markings are different. They live alone in shallow burrows and hunt rodents and rabbits.

51

_small ears_

Carnivores
# OTTER

_short legs_

Otters are playful aquatic mammals. Their large lungs and streamlined bodies enable them to swim fast underwater in search of prey.

_otter in lookout position, balanced on feet and tail_

## COMMON OTTER

A common otter lives by freshwater rivers and lakes across Europe and parts of Asia and Japan. Its home is called a holt. The entrance is in a riverbank, hidden by tree roots.

_chamber above winter flood level_

_underwater entrance_

_strong, tapered tail_

_webbed feet_

When the otter comes out of the water, it shakes itself and rolls around. Then it grooms itself to keep its coat glossy.

Common otters can stay underwater for four minutes. They can see as well underwater as on land.

Common otters are playful both on land and in the water. They make slides on wet or snowy riverbanks.

Common otter cubs do not go into the water until they are about three months old when their coats are waterproof. Their mother has to push them into the water to make them swim.

*body length 1.2m (48in) including tail*

An otter likes to toss a pebble and catch it in its mouth.

A common otter holds its prey while it eats. Its main food is fish.

## SEA OTTER

The sea otter lives in shallow waters off the coasts of California and Alaska. It comes ashore only during storms.

*body length 1.8m (71in) including tail*

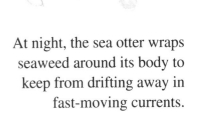

After diving for shellfish, sea urchins and crabs, the sea otter floats on its back to eat.

At night, the sea otter wraps seaweed around its body to keep from drifting away in fast-moving currents.

# RACCOON

*eyes with 'burglar mask'*

*forepaws like hands*

*long, clawed toes*

*thick, striped tail*

At one time, raccoons lived mainly in North American forests, making their dens in tree hollows and rock crevices. But, as woods have been cut down, they have adapted to life in the open country, and even in towns. In towns, they may roam in groups and scavenge to survive. In the wild, raccoons are solitary and jealously guard their food supplies.

*long, thick fur*

*body length 95cm (37in) including tail*

A litter of three to four cubs is born in the spring, fully furred. At first, they are blind and helpless. Their mother suckles them for two months, until they are ready to go foraging.

In times of danger, the mother carries her cubs by the scruff of their necks to a safer place.

Raccoons are very curious, and use
their nimble forepaws to open doors,
turn knobs, and lift dustbin lids.

Raccoons sometimes hunt at night
in shallow water for crustaceans,
molluscs, frogs, and fish. They dabble
underwater with their sensitive fingers until
they find prey. Then they quickly scoop it out.
They also eat earthworms, insects, birds' eggs
and chicks, as well as fruits, nuts and berries.

In cold climates, raccoons grow
a thick coat and gain weight for the winter.
They sleep through the coldest days in their
den. In the southern United States, however,
raccoons stay active all year.

*forepaw*

*hind paw*

*footprints*

55

# CAT

Wild cats survive mainly in remote parts of the world. They are silent, skilful hunters that walk on the pads of their toes to creep up quietly on their prey. Sharp claws and teeth also aid them in catching their prey.

## JUNGLE CAT

*pointed ears*

*forward-facing eyes for judging distances*

*long, sensitive whiskers*

*muscular legs and shoulders*

*claws sheathed when walking*

The jungle cat lives in the forests and grasslands of Asia and the Middle East. It feeds on rodents and birds.

A jungle cat tries to get as close as possible to its prey before it attacks. It flattens itself in the grass and prepares to leap.

It pounces on its prey and catches it with its claws.

## EUROPEAN WILD CAT

The European wild cat is a surprisingly fierce member of the cat family. It is the ancestor of the domestic cat, but it is larger and has much thicker fur. European wild cats live alone in forests and on mountainsides, and hunt at night.

*body length 84cm (33in) including tail*

*forepaw with claws out*

*hind paw with soft pads*

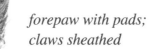

*forepaw with pads; claws sheathed*

Like domestic cats, wild cats often scratch trees to exercise their muscles and sharpen their worn claws.

A female may mate with the same male twice a year. Her kittens are born in a grass-lined den which she makes in a hollow tree or rock crevice.

Kittens chase each other playfully and have mock fights.

## SERVAL

The serval lives on the African savannah. It can run fast and leap high through long grass. It can even catch birds in midair.

*long, sensitive ears for hunting at night*

*short, smooth hair*

*spotted coat provides camouflage*

*body length 91cm (36in) including tail*

*long legs*

57

# HABITATS

**Savannah** grasslands are found in the tropics where rain only ever falls at certain times of the year, and the temperature is high all year round. The tall grasses are ideal feeding grounds for enormous herds of grazing animals.

*Savannah animals: Senegal bushbaby, serval*

**Cultivated grasslands** have been colonised by a few small grazing animals. Since farming restricts plants to a few species, the number of different animals is also limited.

*Cultivated grassland animals: European mole, European rabbit, Eastern cottontail, European brown hare, house mouse, European harvest mouse*

**Australian grasslands** have bushes and trees which provide food and shelter for different sorts of animals. The trees are mainly eucalyptus, which are very tough.

*Australian grassland animals: honey possum, hairy-nosed wombat, koala*

**Prairies** are regions covered with tall, thick grasses. Because there are few trees to provide cover, prairie animals must be constantly on guard for predators. Many animals live in large groups which helps protect them.

*Prairie animals: prairie dog, American badger*

**Temperate woodlands** have a mixture of trees, such as oak, beech, ash and hickory, with shrubs and other plants growing beneath them. In autumn, most of the trees shed their leaves. The forest floor is covered with rotting leaves that teem with worms and insects, providing food for many small mammals.

*Temperate forest animals: brush-tailed possum, Virginia opossum, common shrew, European mole, pipistrelle, greater horseshoe bat, long-eared bat, grey squirrel, flying squirrel, wood mouse, European bank vole, red fox, Eurasian badger, raccoon, jungle cat, European wild cat*

**Evergreen forests** have pine, spruce and fir trees which grow thickly, blocking out the sunlight, so that few plants grow on the forest floor. Animals living here have thick coats to protect them during the bitterly cold, snowy winters.

*Evergreen forest animals: snowshoe hare*

**Tropical rainforests** are found near the Equator where the weather is constantly hot and rainy. In these hot, humid conditions, plants grow fast and provide plenty of food and shelter for the widest variety of animals in the world.

*Tropical rainforest animals: grey-headed fruit bat, squirrel monkey, spider monkey, douroucouli, capuchin monkey, golden lion tamarin, common marmoset, slow loris, ring-tailed lemur*

**Deserts** are dry regions where less than 25cm (10in) of rain falls a year, so very few plants can grow there. Desert animals have found ways to survive without much water.

*Desert animals: numbat, desert jerboa, Mongolian gerbil, kangaroo rat, Eastern woodrat*

**Rivers and streams** provide food and shelter for many small animals whose bodies are streamlined for swimming. Many of them build burrows in the riverbanks and find food in the water.

*River animals: platypus, European water shrew, North American star-nosed mole, marsh cottontail, beaver, European water vole, common otter*

**Suburban gardens** provide refuge for several small animals, which may scavenge in dustbins for food.

*Suburban garden animals: Eurasian badger, raccoon, red fox*

# GLOSSARY

**Adaptation** The way an animal copes efficiently with its environment and so improves its chances of survival.

**Aggressive** Quarrelsome

*red foxes fighting*

**Aquatic** Growing or living in water.

**Breed** To produce young.

**Buck** A male rabbit.

**Camouflage** The way in which an animal's body covering helps it blend into its surroundings so it can hide from enemies or creep up on its prey.

**Canine teeth** The long pointed teeth on either side of the incisor teeth, used for killing and tearing. These are especially prominent in carnivores.

**Carnivore** A mammal that eats the flesh of other animals.

**Colony** A large group of the same species of animals which live together in a fixed home.

**Dependent** Relying on another animal, usually parents, for food and support.

**Doe** A female rabbit.

**Dominant** The dominant animal in a group chooses the best female and has the pick of the available food. Other animals may fight the dominant one for its position of power and importance.

**Forage** Search for food.

**Form** A shallow hole scraped by a rabbit or hare for shelter.

**Groom** To clean by picking deep down in the hair.

*capuchin monkeys*

**Habitat** The surroundings in which an animal lives, such as grassland or desert.

**Herbivore** A mammal that eats plants.

*European rabbit feeding on grass*

**Hibernation** A time of inactivity, rather like a deep sleep, during the cold winter months when there is little or no food available. When an animal hibernates, its breathing and heart rate slow down and its body temperature drops. It uses very little energy and survives on the fat it has built up in its body before hibernation.

**Incisor teeth** The long flat sharp teeth at the front of the mouth, particularly prominent in rodents.

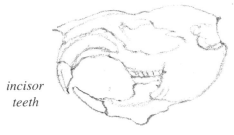

*incisor teeth*

*skull of a beaver*

**Independent** Capable of living alone.

**Invertebrate** An animal without a backbone, such as an earthworm or slug.

**Litter** The babies of a single mother, all born at the same time.

*European wild cat nursing litter*

**Nocturnal** An animal that is active at night and rests during the day.

**Opposable** Thumbs or toes which can move and turn freely, and touch the tips of the other fingers are called opposable. This is a feature of primates.

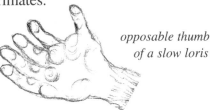

*opposable thumb of a slow loris*

**Paralyse** To make something incapable of moving, usually with a poisonous bite.

**Predator** An animal that hunts and kills other animals for food.

**Prehensile tail** A muscular tail adapted for grasping rather like a hand. It is usually bald on the gripping side.

**Prey** An animal which is hunted and eaten by other animals.

**Roost** A sleeping or resting place.

**Scent gland** A part of the body which produces smelly substances.

**Skull** The bony skeleton protecting the head of a mammal.

*skull of European brown hare*

**Social** Living in a group.

**Solitary** Living alone.

**Species** A kind of animal. Animals of the same species can breed together.

**Streamlined** Shaped to move easily through the water or the air.

**Territory** An area of land which animals mark out as their own and which they defend against other animals of the same species.

**Warren** A network of underground tunnels and chambers in which rabbits live.

*warren of a European rabbit*